MW00571357

CHOCOLATE
CONSPIRACY

COLE GROUP

Both U.S. and metric units are provided for all recipes in this book. Ingredients are listed with U.S. units on the left and metric units on the right. The metric quantities have been rounded for ease of use; as a result, in some recipes there may be a slight difference (approximately $1/2$ ounce or 15 grams) between the portion sizes for the two types of measurements.

© 1995 Cole Group, Inc.

Front cover photograph: Patricia Brabant
Nutritional Analysis: Master Cook II, Arion Software Inc.

Cole Publishing Group, Inc.
1330 N. Dutton Ave., Suite 103
Santa Rosa, CA 95401
(800) 959-2717 (707) 526-2682
FAX (707) 526-2687

Printed in Hong Kong

G F E D C B A
1 0 9 8 7 6 5

ISBN 1-56426-815-2

Library of Congress Catalog Card Number 95-20619

Distributed to the book trade by Publishers Group West

Cole books are available for quantity purchases for sales promotions, premiums, fund-raising, or educational use. For more information on *Chocolate Conspiracy* or other Cole's Cooking Companion books, please write or call the publisher.

CONTENTS

BEHIND THE CONSPIRACY

When chocolate is your obsession, you don't need an excuse to surrender to the consuming passion it inspires. The exquisite pleasures chocolate offers are justification enough to indulge *anytime*—not merely at dessert or on special occasions. *Chocolate Conspiracy* offers more than 50 tempting ways to fulfill a chocolate fancier's fantasies.

About the Recipes

Whether you're craving a dark, sweet little potion to lift you out of the doldrums or a decadent *coup de grâce* to share on a romantic evening, you'll find it in *Chocolate Conspiracy,* with recipes suited to any time of day, any occasion, and any mood. There's even a section devoted to guilt-free gratification for nutrition-minded chocolate lovers. Near the end of each recipe in this special section are listed the number of calories and the amount of fat, percentage of calories from fat, and cholesterol contained in the serving size indicated. Optional ingredients, garnishes, and ingredients used to prepare bakeware are not represented in the nutritional values.

Choosing the Right Chocolate

The food of gods and emperors, chocolate assumes many forms, but all have their origins in the humble fruit of the cacao tree. Fermenting and processing the cocoa beans yields a dark elixir—"chocolate liquor"—that can be transformed into different types of chocolate and chocolate products. Here are some of the most common:

Unsweetened Pure chocolate liquor in solid form, unsweetened chocolate generally is sold in 8-ounce (225 g) packages divided into 1-ounce (30 g) squares for easy measuring. Excellent for truffles, brownies, and sauces, unsweetened chocolate also adds intensity and richness to ice cream and other frozen specialties.

Unsweetened Cocoa Powder Much of the cocoa butter found in solid chocolate is extracted from cocoa powder during processing, rendering it relatively low in fat. It is sold in metal tins or cardboard packages. Never try to substitute "instant cocoa" mixes containing milk solids and sugar or artificial sweeteners for unsweetened cocoa in recipes. You can substitute 3 tablespoons unsweetened cocoa plus a tablespoon of butter or shortening for solid chocolate in most recipes.

Sweetened Sometimes known as *eating chocolate,* sweetened chocolate has cocoa butter and sugar added to it. Sold in paper-wrapped bars, sweetened chocolate can be *bittersweet* (the most intensely flavored and the least sweet) *semisweet,* or *sweet* (the sweetest chocolate). It is also available in chip form, which you can use ounce for ounce in place of bar chocolate. A 6-ounce (170-g) package contains a cup (250 ml) of chips. Sweetened chocolate is used in many baked goods, frozen desserts, and sauces. *Milk chocolate,* which usually contains milk solids, should not be used in recipes unless specified.

White Chocolate A blend of cocoa butter, sugar, milk, and flavorings, this product contains no chocolate liquor; therefore, technically it is not genuine chocolate. Available in bar form, it is used for dipping and decorations and with dark chocolate to provide visual contrast. It should not be used as a substitute for other types of chocolate.

Storing and Working with Chocolate

Storing chocolate properly and handling it with care will help preserve its unique flavor and texture. Tightly wrapped, bar chocolate keeps from 4–12 months, depending upon temperature and humidity. Cocoa stays fresh indefinitely in an airtight tin or jar.

The ideal environment for storing chocolate has a temperature of 78°F (26°C), with low humidity. Chocolate that has been refrigerated sweats when brought to room temperature and may not melt properly. Stored in too warm a place, it may develop a harmless coating (bloom) of cocoa butter on the surface; melting liquifies the cocoa butter and restores chocolate's true color.

When you work with chocolate, pick a cool time of day and keep the room as cool as possible. Melting chocolate requires low heat and your full attention. It burns easily and may become grainy and hard if overheated. Chocolate melts readily in hot liquid, such as milk or cream, if you have at least a tablespoon of liquid per ounce (30 ml) of chocolate.

To melt chocolate by itself, first chop it into small pieces. Once melted, allow chocolate to cool slightly (5–10 minutes) before you use it. For information on tempering chocolate for dipping or decorations, see page 29. Any of the following methods for melting chocolate can produce a smooth, glossy consistency:

Double boiler method: Place chocolate in the top of a double boiler or stainless steel bowl set over a pan of barely simmering (not boiling) water just until chocolate liquifies. For most recipes, there is no need to stir the chocolate as it melts in the double boiler. Moisture from steam or other sources can cause chocolate to seize (tighten) into a hard mass. If this occurs, add a teaspoon of shortening per ounce (30 g) of chocolate to restore smoothness.

Direct-heat method: Place chocolate in a heavy saucepan over very low heat and stir until chocolate liquifies.

Microwave method: Place chocolate in a microwave-safe bowl or cup and set microwave oven on full power. Chocolate will melt in 1–3 minutes, depending on the amount used. If melting more than an ounce (30 g), stir the chocolate once, about halfway through the melting time.

As seductive and enchanting as chocolate is, sometimes it can be temperamental; but if you follow the recipes, techniques, and tips in *Chocolate Conspiracy*, sweet success can be yours.

RECIPES AND TECHNIQUES FOR CHOCOLATE

*T*he collection of recipes and techniques in
Chocolate Conspiracy demonstrates the
incredible variety of captivatingly delicious
creations you can make from chocolate.
Discover the secrets of preparing chocolate-
dipped delicacies, brownies, cookies, truffles,
tortes, bonbons, parfaits, cheesecakes,
mousses, low-fat specialties, and more.

SUDDEN IMPULSE

Satisfy a sudden impulse for something chocolaty with chunky chocolate cookies, chocolate fondue, chocolate-peanut clusters, or sinfully rich truffles. From simple brownies and fudge sauce to double mocha and spiced hot chocolate, this section is devoted to near-instant gratification.

CHOCOLATE-FILLED CHOCOLATE NESTS

Delicate cocoa pastry surrounds a creamy chocolate-raspberry filling.

Cocoa Pastry

1¼ cups	flour	300 ml
2 tbl	unsweetened cocoa	2 tbl
⅓ cup	confectioners' sugar	85 ml
½ cup	cold butter	125 ml
1	egg yolk	1
½ tsp	vanilla extract	½ tsp
⅓ cup	raspberry jam	85 ml
5 oz	semisweet chocolate, coarsely chopped	140 g
3 tbl	sugar	3 tbl
1 tsp	vanilla extract	1 tsp
3 tbl	butter	3 tbl
⅓ cup	whipping cream	85 ml

1. To prepare pastry, in a medium bowl stir together flour, cocoa, and confectioners' sugar. Cut in butter until mixture resembles coarse crumbs. In a small bowl combine egg yolk, vanilla, and ½ tablespoon water; beat until blended. Add egg mixture to flour mixture, stirring with a fork until dough clings together. Press dough into a smooth ball and roll out between 2 sheets of plastic film into a rectangle about 8 by 11 inches (20 by 33 cm). Refrigerate dough until chilled (about 15 minutes).

2. Preheat oven to 350°F (175°C). Remove dough from refrigerator. Working quickly, cut out 2½-inch (6.25-cm) rounds of dough, using a cookie cutter or inverted wine glass. Place rounds over the cup bottoms of inverted miniature (1¾-inch or 4.4-cm) muffin pans, pressing dough to shape "nests." Bake until lightly browned and firm (10–15 minutes).

3. Let nests cool in pans on wire racks. Carefully remove nests from inverted muffin pans. Spoon about ½ teaspoon raspberry jam into each nest.

4. In a heavy saucepan over low heat, combine chocolate, sugar, vanilla, and the 3 tablespoons butter. Heat, stirring occasionally, until chocolate and butter melt and sugar is dissolved. Add cream; stir over medium heat until mixture is hot to the touch (2–3 minutes). Remove from heat and let stand until cooled to room temperature (about 20 minutes).

5. Spoon the chocolate filling into each tart shell. Let stand at room temperature until filling is set (about 1 hour).

Makes 24 pastries.

CHOCOLATE FONDUE

Arrange bowls of fruit and cubes of pound cake for dipping around the fondue pot.

½ cup	whipping cream	125 ml
8 oz	semisweet chocolate, finely chopped	225 g
1 tsp	vanilla extract	1 tsp
2 tbl	rum	2 tbl
1	8 inch- (20 cm-) packaged pound cake	1
2 each	apples and pears	2 each
1	lemon, juiced	1
1 pint	strawberries	500 ml

1. Place cream in fondue pot; slowly heat. When bubbles form around edge, turn off heat and whisk in chocolate until melted; stir in vanilla and rum.

2. Cut pound cake, apples, and pears into 1-inch- (2.5-cm-) square pieces. Drizzle lemon juice over apples and pears. Wash and dry strawberries. Use fondue forks or bamboo skewers to dip fruit and cake into chocolate sauce.

Makes 6 servings.

CHOCOLATE-CHUNK COOKIES

Delectable imported semisweet chocolate, coarsely chopped, transforms ordinary chocolate-chip cookies into chunky ones.

1¼ cups	flour	300 ml
½ tsp	baking soda	½ tsp
¼ tsp	salt	¼ tsp
½ cup	butter, softened	125 ml
½ cup	firmly packed brown sugar	125 ml
½ cup	sugar	125 ml
1	egg	1
1 tsp	vanilla extract	1 tsp
4 oz	semisweet chocolate, coarsely chopped	115 g
½ cup	chopped walnuts (optional)	125 ml

1. In a small bowl stir together flour, baking soda, and salt to combine thoroughly. Set aside.

2. Preheat oven to 375°F (190°C). In a mixing bowl combine butter and sugars; beat until fluffy. Beat in egg. Add vanilla and mix well. Gradually add flour mixture, mixing until just blended. Fold in chocolate and walnuts, if used.

3. Drop by rounded tablespoons, about 1½ inches (3.75 cm) apart, onto lightly oiled baking sheets. Bake until cookies are well browned (12–14 minutes). Cool on wire racks.

Makes about 30 cookies.

COOKIE-BAKING HINTS

- *Transfer drop cookie dough to baking sheet using one tablespoon to scoop the dough and a second to shape it.*

- *Bake one sheet at a time, using the middle rack.*

- *Let baking sheet cool completely between batches or dough will begin to spread excessively before it enters the oven.*

Sour Cream-Chocolate Drops

In making these brownielike cookies, save time by mixing the ingredients in the same saucepan used to melt the butter and chocolate.

1¼ cups	flour	300 ml
½ tsp each	baking powder, baking soda, and ground cinnamon	½ tsp each
¼ tsp	salt	¼ tsp
½ cup	butter	125 ml
3 oz	unsweetened chocolate	85 g
¾ cup	sugar	175 ml
½ cup	firmly packed brown sugar	125 ml
1	egg	1
1 tsp	vanilla extract	1 tsp
½ cup	sour cream	125 ml
¾ cup	chopped pecans	175 ml
as needed	chocolate sprinkles (optional)	as needed

1. In a bowl stir together flour, baking powder, baking soda, cinnamon, and salt to combine thoroughly. Set aside.

2. Preheat oven to 350°F (175°C). In a heavy saucepan over low heat, combine butter and chocolate, stirring occasionally until both are melted.

3. Remove chocolate mixture from heat; stir in sugars. Add egg and vanilla; beat well. Add flour mixture alternately with sour cream, mixing until smooth after each addition. Stir in pecans.

4. Drop by tablespoons, about 1½ inches (3.75 cm) apart, onto lightly oiled baking sheets. Decorate with chocolate sprinkles, if desired. Bake until cookies feel firm when touched lightly (12–14 minutes). Cool on wire racks.

Makes about 42 cookies.

CLASSIC FUDGE BROWNIES

There is very little flour—but lots of chocolate—in these brownies, so they are moist-textured and intensely flavored.

3 oz	unsweetened chocolate	85 g
½ cup	butter	125 ml
⅓ cup	flour	85 ml
½ tsp	baking powder	½ tsp
¼ tsp	salt	¼ tsp
2	eggs, at room temperature	2
½ cup each	sugar and firmly packed brown sugar	125 ml each
1 tsp	vanilla extract	1 tsp
1 cup	coarsely chopped walnuts	250 ml

1. Preheat oven to 350°F (175°C). In a heavy saucepan over low heat, combine chocolate and butter. Let stand until melted, then stir well to blend. Set aside.

2. In a small bowl stir together flour, baking powder, and salt to combine thoroughly. Set aside.

3. In a mixing bowl combine eggs and sugars; beat at high speed until thick. Blend in vanilla, then chocolate mixture. Gradually add flour mixture, beating until well combined. Stir in walnuts.

4. Spread batter in lightly buttered and floured 8-inch- (20-cm-) square pan. Bake until edges pull away from sides of pan and center is nearly set when tested with a toothpick (24–28 minutes). Do not overbake.

5. Let cool in pan on a wire rack (about 10 minutes), then cut into bars. Remove from pan when cool.

Makes 18 brownies.

Cake-Lover's Brownies

The texture of these rich brownies (see photo on page 11) resembles chocolate cake. For an elegant variation, replace the unsweetened chocolate used in this recipe with coarsely chopped white chocolate.

4 oz	unsweetened chocolate, chopped	115 g
½ cup	butter, softened	125 ml
¾ cup	sugar	175 ml
3	eggs	3
1 tbl	vanilla extract	1 tbl
½ cup	flour	125 ml
pinch	salt	pinch
1 cup	chopped pecans or walnuts	250 ml
¼ cup	semisweet chocolate chips (optional)	60 ml

1. Preheat oven to 350°F (175°C). Line bottom of an 8-inch- (20-cm-) square cake pan with parchment paper; lightly butter and flour bottom and sides of pan.

2. In a double boiler over hot (not boiling) water, melt chocolate; remove from heat and cool.

3. In a medium bowl cream together butter and sugar until the consistency of whipped cream. Add eggs, one at a time, beating well after each addition. Stir in vanilla.

4. Sift flour and salt, and fold into egg mixture; gently blend in chocolate, then nuts and chocolate chips, if used. Spread into prepared pan; bake until toothpick inserted in center comes out clean (about 25 minutes). Cool in pan. Refrigerate at least 2 hours before cutting. Serve chilled or at room temperature.

Makes about 16 brownies.

BITTERSWEET CHOCOLATE SAUCE

Here's a chocolate sauce that yields a bittersweet glaze.

3 tbl	sugar	3 tbl
6 oz	semisweet chocolate, coarsely chopped	170 g
2 oz	unsweetened chocolate, coarsely chopped	60 g
1 cup	light whipping cream	250 ml

1. Combine sugar with 3 tablespoons water in a saucepan; bring to a boil over low heat, stirring constantly until sugar dissolves. Remove from heat and cool to 120°F (49°C).

2. Melt chocolate over hot (not boiling) water until just melted. Remove from heat. Pour in sugar syrup all at once. Stir until smooth.

3. Heat cream in a small saucepan over low heat to 120°F (49°C). Pour into chocolate mixture and stir until smooth and shiny. Serve warm.

Makes about 2 cups (500 ml).

CHOCOLATE SODA FOUNTAIN SYRUP

Use this low-fat syrup for chocolate malts and milk shakes.

½ cup	unsweetened cocoa	125 ml
½ cup	sugar	125 ml
½ cup	light corn syrup	125 ml
1 tsp	vanilla extract	1 tsp

In a heavy saucepan over medium heat, combine cocoa and sugar with ½ cup (125 ml) water. Cook, stirring constantly, until cocoa and sugar are dissolved and mixture is smooth. Remove from heat, stir in corn syrup and vanilla, and let cool. Refrigerate until needed.

Makes about 1½ cups (350 ml).

CHOCOLATE-DIPPED FRUIT

Fresh fruit dipped in dark chocolate presents a temptation few can resist. Fruits should be completely dry before dipping. Any residual moisture will cause the chocolate to seize or become stiff. Strawberries, candied citrus peels, and dried figs look fabulous half-dipped into the chocolate. Fruits that tend to darken when exposed to the air—bananas, apples, and pears—or moist fruits— orange sections, raspberries, and seedless grapes—should be completely coated.

After dipping set the fruit on a baking sheet lined with aluminum foil or parchment paper to allow the chocolate coating to harden slightly.

1	seedless orange, peeled and sectioned	1
1	apple, cored and cut into 12 slices	1
1 pint	raspberries	500 ml
14 oz	semisweet chocolate, tempered	400 g
	(see page 29)	

1. Using a dipping fork or your fingers, dip orange sections and apple slices into warm, tempered chocolate. Coat fruit completely, lift from bowl of chocolate, shake gently to remove excess chocolate, and place on a baking sheet lined with aluminum foil or parchment paper. Dip raspberries in same manner, being extremely gentle.

2. Store dipped fruit in the refrigerator, loosely covered, up to 48 hours (12 hours or less for raspberries) if not serving immediately.

Makes about 48 dipped fruits.

STRAWBERRIES IN WHITE CHOCOLATE

Who could resist ripe berries in creamy white chocolate? Because strawberries are highly perishable, they are best eaten within hours after dipping.

30 large	strawberries, with long stems	30 large
10 oz	white chocolate, melted (see below)	285 g

1. If necessary, wash strawberries and thoroughly pat dry. Melt chocolate according to instructions below.

2. Hold strawberries by their stems. Dipping one at a time, lower tip of strawberry into chocolate to cover bottom half of the fruit. Gently shake strawberry to remove excess chocolate and place on a baking sheet lined with aluminum foil or parchment paper. Repeat with remaining strawberries, setting berries about ½ inch (1.25 cm) apart on baking sheet.

3. When chocolate coating has hardened slightly, arrange dipped strawberries on a serving dish. Serve at once or cover and place in refrigerator to chill. Refrigerate fruit no more than 12 hours if not serving immediately.

Makes 30 strawberries.

MELTING WHITE CHOCOLATE

The best method for melting white chocolate (see page 8) requires a double boiler. Heat water in bottom of double boiler just until it boils. Turn off heat and place coarsely chopped chocolate in top of the double boiler. Stir constantly until chocolate is completely melted. Allow chocolate to cool slightly before using.

TOASTED PEANUT CLUSTERS

The winning combination of chocolate and peanuts is further enhanced by butterscotch in this made-in-the-microwave confection that tastes simply delicious! For a delightful variation substitute salted toasted almonds for the peanuts.

2 cups	salted peanuts	500 ml
1 12-oz pkg	semisweet chocolate chips	1 350-g pkg
1 6-oz pkg	butterscotch chips	1 170-g pkg

1. Spread single layer of peanuts in the bottom of a shallow microwave-safe baking dish. Microwave on full power until peanuts are toasted (3–5 minutes), stirring once every minute and watching carefully to prevent nuts from burning. Set toasted peanuts aside.

2. In a 4-cup (900-ml) microwave-safe cup measure, combine chocolate and butterscotch chips. Microwave on full power until chips are melted (2–3 minutes), stirring twice.

3. Add toasted peanuts to chocolate mixture and stir until thoroughly combined. Using a teaspoon, drop toasted peanut mixture into clusters on a baking sheet lined with waxed paper. Let cool until solid (about 15 minutes). Cover and store in refrigerator.

Makes 36 clusters.

CHOCOLATE TRUFFLES

Truffles are extremely easy to make because they have few ingredients and unlike most other candies, don't depend on a temperamental sugar syrup for their base. Note that the truffle mixture must chill overnight before shaping and coating. For a spectacular presentation, serve the edible truffles in cups made of white chocolate (see photo on page 27 and recipe on page 67).

1¼ cups	whipping cream	300 ml
16 oz	semisweet chocolate, coarsely chopped	450 g
½ cup	unsalted butter, cut in small pieces	125 ml
as needed	unsweetened cocoa, chocolate sprinkles, or finely chopped walnuts or pecans for coating	as needed

1. In a heavy saucepan over moderately high heat bring cream to a boil. Add chocolate in small bits. Then add butter, a little at a time, stirring until all is smooth, and remove from heat. Cover and chill 8 hours or overnight.

2. If using cocoa for coating, sift onto a plate. If using sprinkles or nuts, place in a layer on a plate. Scoop up chocolate mixture in teaspoonfuls. Using hands, quickly shape into ¾-inch (1.9-cm) balls (chocolate will melt a bit when handled). Roll in coating and set on another plate. Store, covered, in refrigerator until ready to serve. Truffles keep up to 1 month.

Makes about 72 truffles.

DOUBLE MOCHA

This luscious hot drink makes a brunch treat with brioches and fresh fruit.

2½ tbl	unsweetened cocoa	2½ tbl
¼ cup	sugar	60 ml
pinch	salt	pinch
¼ cup	hot water	60 ml
2 cups	milk	500 ml
¼ tsp	vanilla extract	¼ tsp
2 cups	hot espresso	500 ml
as needed	whipped cream (optional)	as needed

1. In a saucepan stir together cocoa, sugar, and salt. Blend in water. Bring to a boil over medium heat, stirring constantly for 1 minute.

2. Gradually add milk, stirring with a whisk. Heat until cocoa is steaming hot but just under the boiling point. Add vanilla, then beat with whisk until cocoa is frothy. Divide mixture among 4 mugs.

3. Fill mugs to top with espresso. Top each serving with a dollop of whipped cream, if desired.

Serves 4.

FLAVOR PAIRINGS WITH CHOCOLATE

Chocolate blends with many other flavors to create some unique taste sensations. Add a dash of coffee-, mint-, nut-, or fruit-flavored liqueur to plain chocolate cakes and tortes. Blend a bit of Cognac, bourbon, or whisky into the ingredients for chocolate truffles and desserts. Subtle flavor undertones from vanilla, almond, coffee, or mint extract can add interest to chocolate sauces and beverages. Curls of orange zest, sliced almonds, fresh berries, or crumbled praline make flavorful decorations for cakes and tortes.

Tempering Chocolate

Tempering dark chocolate involves heating chocolate and then slightly cooling it by stirring in additional grated chocolate. Using tempered chocolate for dipping (see page 22) or decorations (see page 77) ensures a shiny, unstreaked surface when the chocolate rehardens. The best chocolate for tempering is a semisweet coating chocolate, also called couverture, available from wholesale bakery supply houses.

For every 4 ounces (115 g) of coarsely chopped bittersweet or semisweet chocolate, you will need 1 tablespoon grated chocolate. Melt chopped chocolate in a double boiler over barely simmering water; stir until smooth. Do not allow chocolate to exceed 115°F (46°C) or it will burn. Remove from heat and stir in grated chocolate, 1 tablespoon at a time, stirring well after each addition until chocolate cools to 86°F (30°C).

New Mexico-Style Hot Chocolate

From the American Southwest comes hot chocolate flavored with spices. Try serving it for a weekend brunch, with fresh oranges and an assortment of sweet rolls.

¼ cup each	sugar and unsweetened cocoa	60 ml each
½ tsp	instant coffee granules	½ tsp
⅛ tsp	salt	⅛ tsp
1 stick	cinnamon	1 stick
2 cups	milk	500 ml
1 cup	half-and-half	250 ml
1 tbl	vanilla extract	1 tbl
⅛ tsp	ground cloves	⅛ tsp

1. In a large saucepan mix sugar, cocoa, coffee granules, and salt. Stir in 1 cup (250 ml) water; add cinnamon stick. Bring to a boil, reduce heat, and simmer for 5 minutes.

2. Add milk and half-and-half to cocoa mixture, stirring constantly. Bring to a boil and then remove from heat.

3. Mix in vanilla and cloves; remove cinnamon stick; whisk until foamy, then serve.

Serves 4.

FOR KIDS OF ALL AGES

Bonbons for nibbling at a matinée movie, buttercream-frosted brownies, or ice cream sandwiches even better than those from the ice cream man—sweet memories of childhood are the focus of this section. Kids young and old will enjoy creating their own chocolate fun with recipes that inspire the imagination and thrill the palate.

BONBONS

Simple enough for children to make, bonbons work well with any flavor of ice cream. Peanut butter ice cream is a favorite with many bonbon devotées.

1 pint	ice cream, any flavor	500 ml
12 oz	semisweet chocolate	350 g
2 tbl	unsalted butter	2 tbl

1. Chill a baking sheet lined with waxed paper in the freezer for 20 minutes. With a small ice cream scoop or large melon baller, scoop small balls of ice cream onto sheet. Return sheet to freezer until balls are very firm.

2. In a heavy saucepan over medium heat melt chocolate with butter, stirring until mixture is smooth. Let cool to almost room temperature.

3. Remove ice cream balls from freezer. Insert a fork into one ice cream ball at a time and dip ball into chocolate mixture, covering ball completely; return it to the baking sheet. Work quickly and return bonbons to the freezer as soon as possible. Freeze until solid. Store in covered container until ready to serve.

Makes about 24 bonbons.

CHOCOLATE-ICED BROWNIES

*Chocolate icing and cocoa make these fudgy brownies extra rich.
Microwaving makes them a snap to prepare.*

Chocolate Buttercream Icing

2	egg yolks	2
⅓ cup	sugar	85 ml
½ cup	unsalted butter, softened	125 ml
3 oz	semisweet chocolate, melted and cooled	85 g
½ cup	butter	125 ml
1½ cups	flour	350 ml
1 cup	sugar	250 ml
¼ cup	unsweetened cocoa	60 ml
¼ tsp	salt	¼ tsp
2	eggs, lightly beaten	2
1 tsp	vanilla extract	1 tsp

1. To prepare icing, in a medium bowl, beat yolks until light.
   In a heavy saucepan over medium heat, combine sugar and
   ¼ cup (60 ml) water, stirring until sugar dissolves and syrup
   comes to a boil. Boil without stirring until it reaches 239°F
   (115°C). Remove from heat and pour gradually into yolks,
   beating constantly as you pour. Continue to beat until the
   mixture is light, fluffy, and cool to the touch.

2. In a mixing bowl cream butter. Gradually beat butter into
   yolk mixture, 2 tablespoons at a time, until smooth and
   spreadable. Add chocolate and mix thoroughly. Refrigerate
   until ready to ice brownies.

3. Lightly oil a 9-inch- (22.5-cm-) square microwave-safe
   baking dish. Set aside. In a small microwave-safe bowl,
   microwave butter on full power until melted (1–2 minutes);
   reserve.

4. In a large bowl combine flour, sugar, cocoa, and salt. Add eggs, vanilla, and reserved melted butter, stirring until well mixed.

5. Spread batter in prepared dish. Microwave on full power until top appears dry (6–8 minutes). Let cool directly on heatproof surface. Spread icing on cooled brownies. Cut into squares.

Makes about 16 brownies.

GRASSHOPPER SANDWICHES

The popular combination of chocolate and mint flavors is hard to beat in these fun-to-make ice cream sandwiches.

⅔ cup	flour	150 ml
3 tbl	unsweetened cocoa	3 tbl
¼ tsp each	baking soda and salt	¼ tsp each
½ cup	butter, softened	125 ml
¾ cup	sugar	175 ml
1	egg yolk	1
½ tsp	vanilla extract	½ tsp
1½ cups	quick-cooking rolled oats	350 ml
1 oz	semisweet chocolate	30 g
½ tsp	oil	½ tsp
1 quart	mint chocolate-chip ice cream	900 ml

1. In a bowl stir together flour, cocoa, baking soda, and salt to combine thoroughly. Set aside.

2. In a mixing bowl combine butter and sugar; beat until fluffy. Beat in egg yolk. Add vanilla and mix to blend.

3. Add flour mixture alternately with about 2 tablespoons water, blending until smooth after each addition. Stir in rolled oats. Cover with plastic film and refrigerate until firm (about 1 hour).

4. Preheat oven to 350°F (175°C). On a lightly floured surface, roll out dough to a thickness of about ⅛ inch (.3 cm). Cut out 30 cookies with a 2½-inch- (6.25-cm-) diameter cutter. Transfer to ungreased baking sheets.

5. Bake until cookies are barely firm when centers are touched lightly (8–10 minutes). Let stand on baking sheets about 1–2 minutes, then remove to wire racks to cool.

6. While cookies are cooling, melt semisweet chocolate with oil in a heavy saucepan over low heat. Over half the cookies drizzle melted chocolate.

7. With an ice cream scoop, place 15 mounds of ice cream on a baking sheet and allow to soften slightly. Use a spatula to flatten each scoop to about a 3-inch- (7.5-cm-) diameter disk. Return ice cream to freezer until solidly frozen (1–2 hours).

8. To assemble sandwiches place plain cookies, smooth sides up, in rows on a shallow-rimmed baking sheet. Place a disk of the ice cream atop each. Cover each with a chocolate-drizzled cookie, chocolate side up. Return to freezer until ice cream sandwiches are solidly frozen (1–2 hours). To store, wrap each sandwich in foil and store in freezer for up to 2 months.

Makes 15 ice cream sandwiches.

CHOCOLATE PRETZELS

These trompe l'oeil cookie pretzels speckled with coarse sugar go well with coffee or hot chocolate.

1²/₃ cups	flour	400 ml
¼ cup	unsweetened cocoa	60 ml
¾ cup	butter, softened	175 ml
¾ cup	sugar	175 ml
1 tsp	vanilla extract	1 tsp
1	egg white, lightly beaten	1
2 tbl	coarse (decorating) sugar	2 tbl

1. In a bowl stir together flour and cocoa to combine well. Set aside.

2. In a mixing bowl combine butter and sugar; beat until fluffy. Blend in vanilla. Gradually add flour mixture, beating until smooth. Gather dough into a ball and enclose in plastic film. Refrigerate until firm enough to shape (about 45 minutes).

3. Preheat oven to 350°F (175°C). Work with one fourth of the dough at a time, refrigerating the remainder. Divide each portion into 8 equal pieces. On a lightly floured surface, roll each piece into an 8-inch- (20-cm-) long strand and twist into pretzel shape. Place cookies about 1 inch (2.5 cm) apart on lightly oiled baking sheets. Lightly brush each cookie with beaten egg white, then scatter coarse sugar over surface.

4. Bake until cookies feel firm when touched lightly (12–14 minutes). Let stand on baking sheets about 2 minutes, then transfer to wire racks to cool completely.

Makes about 32 cookies.

CHOCOLATE-MOCHA BROWNIE PIZZA

The mock pizza in the photo features peanut-butter and mocha ice cream, but you can pick your own favorite flavors.

16 oz	semisweet chocolate, coarsely chopped	450 g
¼ cup	unsweetened cocoa	60 ml
4 tbl	unsalted butter	4 tbl
5	eggs	5
1½ cups	sugar	350 ml
1½ tsp	vanilla extract	1½ tsp
1 cup	sifted flour	250 ml
½ tsp	baking powder	½ tsp
pinch	salt	pinch
6 oz each	chocolate chips and chopped walnuts	170 g each
1 qt each	chocolate and mocha ice cream	900 ml each
1 recipe	Hot Fudge Sauce (page 43)	1 recipe
as needed	assorted dessert toppings (optional)	as needed

1. Preheat oven to 350°F (175°C). In a heavy saucepan over low heat, melt semisweet chocolate, cocoa, and 4 tablespoons butter, stirring until smooth. Remove from heat and let mixture cool about 5 minutes.

2. In a large bowl beat eggs and sugar with an electric mixer until thick and pale. Stir in vanilla and cooled chocolate mixture; blend well and set aside.

3. Combine flour, baking powder, and salt. Add to chocolate mixture, stirring just to combine. Fold in chocolate chips and nuts. Spread mixture in buttered pizza pan. Bake 30 minutes, then remove from oven. Meanwhile, remove chocolate ice cream from freezer to soften. Spread pizza with softened chocolate ice cream and dot with scoops of mocha ice cream. Serve with fudge sauce and toppings, if desired.

Makes one 16-inch (40-cm) brownie pizza.

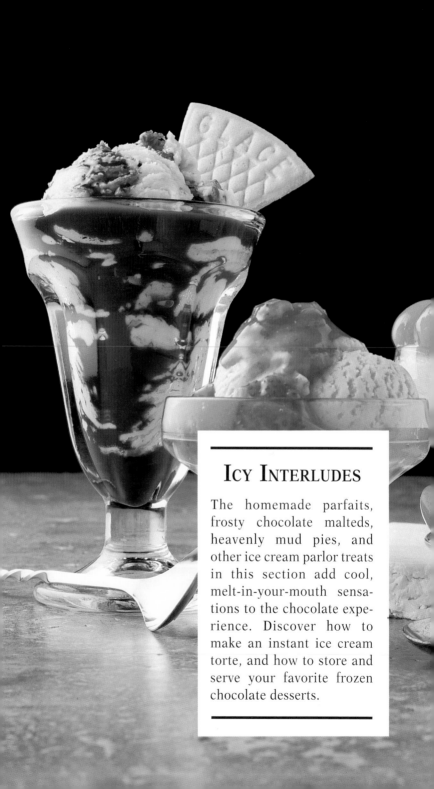

Icy Interludes

The homemade parfaits, frosty chocolate malteds, heavenly mud pies, and other ice cream parlor treats in this section add cool, melt-in-your-mouth sensations to the chocolate experience. Discover how to make an instant ice cream torte, and how to store and serve your favorite frozen chocolate desserts.

HOT FUDGE PARFAIT

This elegantly simple creation is just the thing for a make-your-own parfait or sundae buffet, with guests creating their own desserts from an assortment of ice cream flavors and toppings. The sauce is the old-fashioned type that slides down the ice cream and hardens.

1 quart	butter-pecan ice cream	900 ml

Hot Fudge Sauce

6 tbl	unsalted butter	6 tbl
4 oz	unsweetened chocolate	115 g
1 cup	sugar	250 ml
3 tbl	light corn syrup	3 tbl
1/8 tsp	salt	1/8 tsp
2 tsp	vanilla extract	2 tsp

1. Remove ice cream from the freezer and allow to soften slightly while you make the sauce.

2. In a heavy saucepan over medium heat, melt butter in 1/2 cup (125 ml) water. Bring to a boil, stirring constantly.

3. Add chocolate, stirring occasionally until it melts. (Chocolate may lump; it will smooth out later.)

4. Add sugar, corn syrup, and salt. Boil 5 minutes. Remove from heat and add vanilla. Keep warm.

5. For each parfait, place a scoop of ice cream in a tall glass. Top with 2 tablespoons sauce. Alternate as many layers of ice cream and sauce as desired or as many as the glass will hold.

Serves 4.

PROFITEROLES WITH BITTERSWEET CHOCOLATE SAUCE

Imagine a mound of tiny cream puffs filled with your favorite ice cream and covered with warm Bittersweet Chocolate Sauce (see photo on page 4).

Cream Puff Pastry

4 tbl	unsalted butter, cut into pieces	4 tbl
¼ tsp	salt	¼ tsp
½ tsp	sugar	½ tsp
½ cup	unbleached flour	125 ml
2	eggs	2
1	egg, lightly beaten with 1 teaspoon water (egg wash)	1
1 pint	vanilla or coffee ice cream	500 ml
1 recipe	Bittersweet Chocolate Sauce (see page 20)	1 recipe

1. Preheat oven to 425°F (220°C). Place butter, salt, sugar, and ½ cup (125 ml) water in a saucepan; bring to a boil over low heat. When mixture boils, remove from heat immediately and add flour all at once. Stir vigorously. Return to heat; stir over medium heat until mixture pulls away from sides of pan and just forms a ball (about 30 seconds).

2. Remove from heat; allow to cool 5 minutes. Add eggs, one at a time, beating thoroughly after each addition. The paste should look smooth and shiny.

3. Line baking sheets with parchment paper. Using a spoon, drop 1-inch (2.5-cm) mounds of pastry onto paper-lined baking sheets at least ½ inch (1.25 cm) apart. Brush each puff with egg wash while flattening the top slightly.

4. Bake for 10 minutes. Reduce oven to 400°F (205°C) and bake until crisp and brown (about 10 minutes longer). With tip of knife cut a ⅛-inch (.3-cm) hole in bottom of each puff to release steam. Turn off oven. Return baking sheets to oven and, with door propped slightly ajar, allow cream puffs to dry. When dry, remove from oven and finish cooling on wire racks.

5. Place a baking sheet in freezer to chill. To fill pastries, slice each puff in half horizontally. Form 48 tiny mounds (1 rounded teaspoon each) of ice cream on the sheet. Freeze until solid. Fill bottom half of each shell with one of the ice cream mounds, then put top half of shell on top. Place 6–8 filled profiteroles in each dessert bowl. Pour warm Bittersweet Chocolate Sauce over puffs. Serve immediately.

Makes 8 servings, 6 puffs each.

FROZEN CHOCOLATE BANANAS

Chocolate-covered bananas, frozen on ice cream sticks or wooden skewers, make a refreshing pick-me-up on summer evenings or any other time.

6	firm bananas	6
12 oz	semisweet chocolate	350 g
2 tbl	shortening	2 tbl
as needed	toppings, such as shredded coconut, chopped nuts, sprinkles, or granola (optional)	as needed

1. Peel bananas and halve them crosswise. Insert a stick into the cut end of each banana half and push it in half the length of the fruit. Place bananas on a baking sheet lined with waxed paper and freeze until hard. (Bananas must be frozen or chocolate will not adhere to them.)

2. In a heavy saucepan over moderate heat, melt chocolate with shortening, stirring until mixture is smooth. Let cool slightly (about 2–3 minutes).

3. Remove bananas from freezer. Dip each into chocolate mixture, turning to coat completely. Use a spatula to help coat bananas, if necessary. Roll chocolate-covered bananas in toppings, if desired. Replace on baking sheet.

4. Return to freezer. When chocolate and toppings are firm, wrap each chocolate-dipped banana tightly in plastic film and store in freezer. Let thaw a few minutes before serving.

Makes 12 bananas.

INSTANT ICE CREAM TORTES

Create a distinctive build-it-yourself torte by combining your favorite flavors of ice cream and toppings with an 8-inch (20-cm) sponge cake from the bakery or supermarket. Pair white sponge cake with rocky road ice cream and brandied cherries, chocolate-chip ice cream and raspberry topping, or butter-pecan ice cream and fudge topping. Try chocolate sponge cake with peppermint-stick ice cream and peppermint topping, toffee-crunch ice cream and butterscotch topping, or fudge-ripple ice cream and strawberry topping.

1. *Slice sponge cake in half horizontally. Spread a pint of softened ice cream evenly over the bottom layer. Lay the second layer on top, pressing down to make the cake even. Wrap tightly in plastic film and freeze.*

2. *Remove cake from freezer about 10 minutes before serving. Drizzle topping of your choice over the torte and pass extra topping at the table.*

MUD PIE

This is a favorite among coffee fanatics and chocolate lovers. To make the crust, press a second pie plate directly onto the crumbs for 1–2 minutes to pack them before baking.

Chocolate Cookie Crust

1 pkg (8½ oz)	chocolate wafers, finely crushed	1 pkg (240 g)
6 tbl	unsalted butter, melted	6 tbl
pinch	ground cinnamon	pinch

1 recipe	Hot Fudge Sauce (see page 43)	1 recipe
1 quart	coffee ice cream, softened	900 ml
¾ cup	whipping cream	175 ml
1 tsp	vanilla extract	1 tsp
1 tbl	confectioners' sugar	1 tbl
⅓ cup	toasted almonds, for decorating	85 ml

1. Preheat oven to 350°F (175°C). Butter the bottom, but not the sides, of a 9-inch (22.5-cm) pie plate. In a medium bowl combine crushed wafers, melted butter, and cinnamon. Press crumb mixture evenly into pie plate. Bake on center oven rack 8–10 minutes. Cool to room temperature.

2. Pour a thin layer of warm fudge sauce into the cooled crust and freeze until firm.

3. Spoon ice cream into the frozen crust and smooth the top. Press plastic film over ice cream and freeze at least 1½ hours.

4. Spread a generous layer of fudge sauce over ice cream. Freeze at least 30 minutes. Meanwhile, whip the cream with vanilla and sugar. Spread over the frozen pie. Decorate with toasted almonds and freeze another 2 hours or longer before serving.

Serves 8.

CHOCOLATE MALTED

Here is the best-loved malted of all. The richness of the chocolate blends smoothly with the taste of malted milk powder, available in many supermarkets and natural food stores. To make your own homemade ice cream start with the French Vanilla Ice Cream Base from the recipe on page 53, transfer to an ice cream machine, and freeze according to manufacturer's instructions.

2 scoops	French vanilla ice cream	2 scoops
1 cup	milk	250 ml
2 tbl	malted milk powder	2 tbl
¼ cup	Chocolate Soda Fountain Syrup (see page 20)	60 ml

Combine all ingredients and mix well in a blender. Serve in a chilled glass.

Serves 1.

FROZEN CHOCOLATE ESPRESSO

This offering is bound to bring a smile to anyone who enjoys the combination of coffee and chocolate flavors.

3 oz	semisweet chocolate	85 g
3 tbl	coffee-flavored liqueur	3 tbl
6	eggs, separated	6
¾ cup	sugar	175 ml
2 tbl	instant espresso granules	2 tbl
1 tsp	vanilla extract	1 tsp
1½ cups	whipping cream	350 ml
2 oz	bittersweet chocolate, grated	60 g
as needed	candied coffee beans, for garnish	as needed

1. In a heavy saucepan over low heat, melt chocolate with liqueur and 3 tablespoons water. Let cool slightly. In a medium bowl cream together egg yolks, sugar, espresso granules, and vanilla. Add melted chocolate and mix well.

2. Whip the cream until soft peaks form. Fold into chocolate mixture.

3. Beat egg whites until stiff peaks form; do not let them dry out. Fold in chocolate mixture. Pour into an 8-cup (1.8-l) soufflé dish or 8 individual 1-cup (250-ml) ramekins. Sprinkle grated chocolate on top and garnish with candied coffee beans. Freeze until firm (at least 4 hours).

Serves 8.

FROZEN CHOCOLATE FROMAGE

This very rich dessert resembles a frozen chocolate cheesecake.

6 oz	cream cheese, at room temperature	170 g
2	egg yolks	2
2 tbl	sugar	2 tbl
½ tsp	vanilla extract	½ tsp
1 tbl	coffee-flavored liqueur	1 tbl
½ cup	whipping cream	125 ml
3 oz	semisweet chocolate, melted	85 g
½ cup	slivered almonds, toasted	125 ml

1. In a food processor or blender, mix together cream cheese, egg yolks, sugar, vanilla, liqueur, and cream. When well mixed, blend in melted chocolate. Mix in almonds.

2. Transfer to a 2-cup (500-ml) bowl or four parfait dishes and freeze until firm. Let stand at room temperature for 5 minutes before serving.

Serves 4.

STORING AND SERVING FROZEN DESSERTS

Homemade ice cream and other frozen chocolate desserts should be stored at low temperatures to protect their delicate flavor and texture (10°F or –18°C or lower is ideal). Homemade ice cream should be kept for no more than a day or two. Before serving, warm frozen desserts slightly by transferring them to the refrigerator for 20–30 minutes or leaving them at room temperature for 10–15 minutes. Repeated thawing and refreezing will destroy the texture of frozen desserts, so thaw just until softened to your liking.

DARK CHOCOLATE ICE CREAM

Creamy peaks of velvety dark chocolate make this homemade ice cream an unforgettable experience.

French Vanilla Ice Cream Base

3 cups	whipping cream	700 ml
1 cup	milk	250 ml
¾ cup	sugar	175 ml
4	egg yolks	4
1 tbl	vanilla extract	1 tbl
5 oz	semisweet chocolate	140 g
3 oz	unsweetened chocolate	85 g

1. In a heavy saucepan, heat cream, milk, and sugar. Stir occasionally until sugar is dissolved and the mixture is hot (not boiling).

2. Whisk egg yolks together in a bowl. Continue whisking and very slowly pour in approximately 1 cup (250 ml) of the cream mixture. When smooth, pour back into the pan. Whisk constantly over low heat until the mixture thickens slightly and coats the back of a spoon (about 5 minutes). Do not boil or custard will curdle.

3. Add vanilla extract and strain custard into a clean bowl.

4. Melt chocolates together in a double boiler. Add ½ cup (125 ml) of warm ice cream base to melted chocolate, whisking constantly to keep chocolate smooth. Return mixture to ice cream base, mix well, and let cool.

5. Transfer to an ice cream machine and freeze according to manufacturer's instructions.

Makes about 1 quart (900 ml).

BROWNIE À LA MODE

For a chocolate lover's fantasy place layers of rich brownie and ice cream together in a stemmed dish; then pour on the hot fudge sauce.

1 recipe	Cake-Lover's Brownies	1 recipe
	(see page 19)	
1 pint	vanilla or any other flavor ice cream	500 ml
1 recipe	Hot Fudge Sauce (see page 43)	1 recipe
1 cup	toasted pecans (optional)	250 ml

After baking brownies cut into 16 squares. Place one square in a serving dish, top with a scoop of vanilla ice cream, place a second brownie on the ice cream, top with another small scoop of ice cream, and drizzle with fudge sauce. Repeat with remaining brownies, ice cream, and sauce. Sprinkle with toasted pecans, if desired, and serve at once.

Serves 8.

ELEGANT ENDINGS

When graciously presented, chocolate is the ultimate expression of good taste and celebration. Special occasions and intimate moments deserve the elegance of chocolate. Along with techniques for making chocolate tortes, cakes, cheesecakes, and other fancy desserts, this chapter reveals the secrets of making edible decorations to crown your masterpieces.

BROWNIE FANTASY TORTE

This moist, dense triple-chocolate brownie confection is reminiscent of the renowned Sachertorte.

1 recipe	Cocoa Pastry (see page 13)	1 recipe
½ cup	apricot jam or preserves	125 ml
3 oz	unsweetened chocolate	85 g
½ cup	butter	125 ml
⅓ cup	flour	85 ml
¼ tsp	baking powder	¼ tsp
⅛ tsp	salt	⅛ tsp
2	eggs, at room temperature	2
1 cup	sugar	250 ml
1 tsp	vanilla extract	1 tsp
⅓ cup	sliced almonds	85 ml
1 oz	semisweet chocolate	30 g
½ tsp	oil	½ tsp
as needed	whipped cream (optional)	as needed

1. Preheat oven to 350°F (175°C). Press Cocoa Pastry firmly over bottom and up sides of an 11-inch (27.5-cm) springform tart pan. Bake for 12 minutes. Remove from oven and cool in pan on a wire rack. When pastry is cool to the touch, spread apricot jam evenly over bottom of pastry shell. Set aside.

2. In a heavy saucepan over low heat, combine unsweetened chocolate and butter. Let stand until melted, then stir well to blend. Let cool.

3. In a small bowl stir together flour, baking powder, and salt. Set aside.

4. In a mixing bowl combine eggs and sugar; beat at high speed until thick. Blend in vanilla, then chocolate mixture. Gradually add flour mixture, beating until well combined. Stir in almonds.

5. Spread batter in jam-lined pastry. Return to 350°F (175°C) oven and bake until center is nearly set when tested with a toothpick (20–25 minutes). Remove from oven and let cool in pan on a wire rack. Then carefully remove sides of pan and transfer to a serving plate.

6. In a heavy saucepan over low heat, melt semisweet chocolate with oil. Drizzle melted chocolate over surface of torte. Set aside until chocolate is firm. To serve, cut torte into wedges. Accompany with whipped cream (if desired).

Makes 8 servings.

POTS DE CRÈME PRESTO

These sinfully rich yet not too sweet dessert cups are great for entertaining because they take so little time to make. They can be prepared up to a day ahead if kept covered and refrigerated.

7 oz	unsweetened chocolate	200 g
1 can (14 oz)	sweetened condensed milk	1 can (400 g)
3 tbl	orange liqueur	3 tbl
1½ cups	whipping cream	350 ml

1. Heat chocolate and sweetened condensed milk in double boiler or a bowl set over a pan of hot water. Stir until chocolate melts and mixture is blended.

2. Stir in liqueur, adjusting to taste, and let mixture cool to lukewarm. Whip cream until soft peaks form. Stir about a fourth of the whipped cream into chocolate to lighten mixture. Then fold in all but one large spoonful of remaining whipped cream. Refrigerate remaining cream to decorate tops.

3. Spoon about ½ cup (125 ml) of the mixture each into individual soufflé cups or small dessert dishes. Chill about 30 minutes. Decorate each serving with a dollop of reserved whipped cream.

Makes 8 servings.

Making Chocolate Leaves, Curls, and Shells

Dress up cakes and tortes with chocolate leaves and curls; fill the shells with white chocolate mousse (see page 69).

Leaves Choose thick, waxy non-toxic plant leaves with visible veins such as rose leaves. Brush melted chocolate evenly on underside of leaves. Chill in refrigerator until chocolate is firm. Slide fingernail between leaf and chocolate near stem to loosen chocolate. Pull leaf away from chocolate.

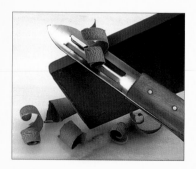

Curls Use a 4-ounce (115 g) or larger bar of chocolate (at room temperature). Scrape the long side of the bar with a sharp vegetable peeler. If chocolate is just the right temperature, you will have nice chocolate curls. If chocolate is too cold, you will end up with short chocolate shavings or shredded chocolate.

Shells Cover the backs of two 5-inch (12.5 cm) scallop shells with a layer of plastic film and then a layer of foil, pressing foil firmly against ridges. Lightly brush foil with oil and place on baking sheet. Melt chocolate in the top of a double boiler. Spoon melted chocolate over the shells, smoothing with a knife. Store in a cool place until hard (at least 2 hours). Carefully separate chocolate shells from foil and plastic, then trim edges.

CHOCOLATE SOUFFLÉ

Sprinkle confectioners' sugar over this light dessert soufflé for a stunning presentation.

1 cup	milk	250 ml
3	egg yolks	3
6 tbl	sugar	6 tbl
4 tbl	flour	4 tbl
2 tsp	vanilla extract	2 tsp
4 oz	semisweet chocolate, melted	125 ml
5	egg whites	5
as needed	confectioners' sugar	as needed

1. Set aside 2 tablespoons of the milk. Bring remaining milk to a boil in a heavy saucepan.

2. In a medium bowl whisk egg yolks lightly. Add 4 tablespoons of the sugar and reserved milk and whisk until thick and smooth. Stir in flour with whisk. Gradually whisk in half the hot milk. Return mixture to milk in saucepan and whisk over low heat until mixture comes to a boil. Remove from heat and whisk in vanilla and chocolate.

3. Preheat oven to 425°F (220°C). Generously butter a 5-cup (1.1-l) soufflé dish.

4. Beat egg whites until stiff. Add remaining sugar, beating at high speed for about 30 seconds. Stir about one quarter of whites into chocolate mixture, spoon over remaining egg whites, and fold together just until blended.

5. Transfer mixture to buttered soufflé dish and quickly smooth top with spatula. Bake until puffed and browned (about 15 minutes). Set soufflé dish on serving platter, sprinkle with confectioners' sugar, and serve.

Serves 4.

Mocha Bavarian Pie

Freshly brewed coffee and dark chocolate blend to produce this mocha cream pie (see photo on page 10).

1 recipe	Chocolate Cookie Crust (see page 48)	1 recipe
4 tsp	unflavored gelatin	4 tsp
⅓ cup	cold coffee or water	85 ml
3	egg yolks	3
as needed	sugar	as needed
1¼ cups	strong, freshly brewed hot coffee	300 ml
2 oz	semisweet chocolate, grated	60 g
1 cup	whipping cream	250 ml
2	egg whites	2
1 tbl	coffee-flavored liqueur	1 tbl
2 recipes	Chantilly Cream (see page 80)	2 recipes
as needed	candied coffee beans (optional)	as needed

1. Prepare crust. Sprinkle gelatin over the ⅓ cup (85 ml) cold coffee in a bowl. Set aside until soft and spongy.

2. Beat egg yolks and ½ cup (125 ml) of the sugar until thick and light-colored.

3. Stir the 1¼ cups (300 ml) hot coffee into yolk mixture; transfer to a saucepan or double boiler. Stir in the 2 ounces (60 g) grated chocolate. Cook over low heat, stirring constantly with a wooden spoon, until the custard thickens slightly and coats the back of spoon (about 5 minutes). Do not boil or custard will curdle.

4. Stir softened gelatin into hot coffee mixture; transfer to a medium bowl. Place bowl over ice water, stirring frequently, until mixture thickens to the consistency of whipped cream.

5. While custard is thickening, whip cream until soft peaks form; refrigerate.

6. Wait to beat the egg whites until just before the coffee mixture reaches the right consistency (see Beating and Folding Egg Whites below). Beat the whites until soft peaks form; beat in 2 tablespoons sugar, 1 tablespoon at a time. Beat until whites form stiff peaks but are still glossy and smooth.

7. When coffee mixture is the consistency of softly whipped cream, stir in the coffee liqueur; fold in the whipped cream, then fold in the egg whites. These steps should be accomplished quickly to prevent the mixture from setting too rapidly.

8. Pour mixture into prepared crust; refrigerate 2 hours or until filling is firm. Decorate pie with Chantilly Cream and candied coffee beans, if used.

Serves 8.

BEATING AND FOLDING EGG WHITES

Beaten egg whites add lightness to cakes and chilled desserts such as mousses. For best results, separate the eggs when you begin the recipe and set aside at room temperature until ready to use. Beat egg whites just until stiff peaks form, but not until they are lumpy or dry. If sugar is to be added, beat just until the whites are shiny. Beaten egg whites lose their volume rapidly if allowed to stand, so use immediately. To combine with other ingredients, gently fold about a quarter of the whites into the heavier mixture. Then fold in remaining egg whites. Careful folding keeps the whipped ingredients from deflating.

White Chocolate Tart

Served with a bowl of fresh raspberry sauce, this wonderful dessert would be a hit at a bridal shower or summer luncheon.

Nut Crust

1	egg	1
5 oz	almonds, finely chopped	140 g
½ cup	unsalted butter, at room temperature	125 ml
3 tbl	sugar	3 tbl
1¼ cups	flour	300 ml
½ tsp	almond extract	½ tsp
¼ tsp	vanilla extract	¼ tsp
pinch	salt	pinch

White Chocolate Mousse

9 oz	white chocolate, finely chopped	255 g
1½ cups	whipping cream	350 ml
2 oz	semisweet chocolate, melted	60 g
as needed	shaved white chocolate, candied violets, and fresh mint leaves, for garnish	as needed

1. Preheat oven to 350°F (175°C). Lightly oil an 11-inch (27.5-cm) tart pan. For crust, beat egg; divide in half and reserve half for another use. In a food processor or blender, combine half of egg and remaining ingredients. When well mixed, press evenly into tart pan. Chill at least 30 minutes. Bake until the edges of the crust pull away from the sides of the pan (20–25 minutes). Transfer pan to a wire rack and cool.

2. For mousse, heat chocolate with ¼ cup (60 ml) water in a double boiler just until chocolate melts. Remove from heat and cool to room temperature. In a separate bowl whip the

cream until soft peaks form. Combine one third of the cream with the melted chocolate, then fold in remaining whipped cream. Pour into a bowl and chill at least 3 hours.

3. To assemble, paint the inside of the crust with the melted chocolate. Pour in the mousse and smooth it. Garnish the top of the tart with shaved white chocolate, candied violets, and fresh mint leaves.

Serves 8.

CHOCOLATE DECADENCE

This intensely rich dessert truly lives up to its name.

20 oz	bittersweet chocolate, coarsely chopped	570 g
½ cup each	rum and cognac	125 ml each
2 cups	whipping cream	500 ml
4	egg whites	4
6	egg yolks	6
¼ cup	sugar	60 ml
¾ cup	coffee or espresso, brewed and cooled	175 ml

1. Generously butter the bottom and sides of a 9-inch (22.5-cm) springform pan. Wrap outside of pan with plastic film and then foil. Place buttered springform pan into a larger cake pan. Set aside.

2. Preheat oven to 325°F (160°C). Place chocolate in bowl and melt over hot water. Combine rum and cognac in a small saucepan and simmer until reduced by half.

3. Beat the cream until stiff peaks form and set aside in refrigerator. Beat egg whites until stiff peaks form and set aside in refrigerator.

4. In a large mixing bowl, beat egg yolks and sugar until pale and thickened (about 2 minutes). Continue to beat on high while slowly adding the reduced rum mixture. Beat until volume triples (about 10 minutes).

5. Into the yolk mixture fold melted chocolate, alternating with coffee. Fold in egg whites and then whipped cream. Pour into prepared pan. Into larger pan pour 1 inch (2.5 cm) of water to make a water bath. Bake until center jiggles but is no longer liquid and edges are dry (about 1¼ hours).

6. Carefully remove to rack to cool; cover and refrigerate several hours or overnight before serving.

Serves 16.

TRUFFLE CUPS

Simple and quick to make, these charming chocolate cups make appealing containers for ice cream and sorbet, fresh fruit, or chocolate truffles (see recipe on page 26). For white truffle cups like the ones shown on page 27, substitute 6 oz (170 g) of white chocolate for the semisweet chocolate and add 4 teaspoons of vegetable shortening.

6 oz	semisweet chocolate, finely chopped	170 g

1. Melt chocolate in a double boiler or a bowl set over a pan of hot water. Stir until smooth.

2. Working quickly, use the back of a spoon or a small knife to spread chocolate on bottom and up sides of 6 standard or 12 miniature cupcake liners. Set liners in a muffin pan. Chill until firm in freezer 10–15 minutes, or in refrigerator 20–30 minutes. Carefully peel off the paper liners, handling chocolate as little as possible. Place on a plate, wrap tightly in plastic film to prevent moisture condensation, and store up to 5 days in refrigerator.

Makes 6 standard or 12 miniature truffle cups.

CHOCOLATE-MINT ROULADE

The mint filling in this microwaved cake roll is a pleasant surprise.
Allow at least an hour for the cake to chill before serving it.

2 recipes	Chantilly Cream (see page 80)	2 recipes
4	eggs	4
¾ cup each	sugar and flour	175 ml each
¼ cup	unsweetened cocoa	60 ml
¾ tsp	baking powder	¾ tsp
1 tsp	vanilla extract	1 tsp
2 tbl	confectioners' sugar, for sprinkling towel	2 tbl
1 box (5½ oz)	chocolate-covered mint patties	1 box (155 g)

1. Prepare Chantilly Cream and refrigerate. Line an 8- by 12-inch (20- by 30-cm) microwave-safe dish with waxed paper cut to fit. Set aside. In a large bowl beat eggs until thick and lemon colored. Add sugar, flour, cocoa, baking powder, and vanilla. Beat until well blended.

2. Pour batter into prepared dish and spread evenly. Microwave on full power 2 minutes. To prevent uneven cooking shield corners of dish with 2-inch- (5-cm-) wide strips of aluminum foil and microwave again on full power until surface appears dry (3–4 minutes).

3. Lay a clean dish towel on a work surface; sprinkle towel with confectioners' sugar. Immediately turn out cake onto sugared towel and remove waxed paper from cake. Roll up cake, starting at long edge. Let cool while rolled.

4. In a small microwave-safe bowl, microwave mint patties on full power until soft (1–2 minutes). Stir until smooth. Unroll cake and spread with melted mint mixture. Spread Chantilly Cream over filling. Roll up filled cake and chill at least 1 hour before serving.

Serves 6.

CHOCOLATE-HAZELNUT GÂTEAU

Layers of hazelnut cake and buttercream create a striking ribbon effect in this elegant cake.

1¼ cups	skinned, finely ground hazelnuts	300 ml
1 cup	sugar	250 ml
3	eggs	3
1 tsp	vanilla extract	1 tsp
3	egg whites	3
⅛ tsp	cream of tartar	⅛ tsp
⅓ cup	sifted cake flour	85 ml
2 tbl	dark rum	2 tbl
½ cup	whipping cream	125 ml
3 recipes	Chocolate Buttercream Icing (see page 34)	3 recipes
as needed	semisweet Chocolate Leaves (see page 60)	as needed

1. Preheat oven to 450°F (230°C). Butter and flour the sides of an 11- by 17-inch (27.5- by 42.5-cm) jellyroll pan. Line bottom of pan with parchment paper cut to fit.

2. Combine ground hazelnuts and ⅓ cup (85 ml) of the sugar in a medium bowl. Add eggs, one at a time, beating well after each addition. Continue beating until creamy (about 5 minutes). Beat in vanilla.

3. In a separate bowl, beat egg whites until foamy; add cream of tartar and beat until soft peaks form. Gradually add ⅓ cup (85 ml) of the sugar and beat until stiff but still glossy. Fold one fourth of the whites into the hazelnut mixture. Then fold in the flour. When flour is well incorporated, carefully fold in the remaining whites. Spread the batter evenly in pan. Bake until light brown and springy to the touch (about 10 minutes).

4. Cool cake in pan 5 minutes. Run a knife along edge to loosen. Remove cake from pan; slide onto wire rack,

paper-side down, and cool. Cover with a clean towel while cooling. Carefully peel paper off cake. Cut the cake into four equal pieces (4 by 11 inches or 10 by 27.5 cm each). Wrap pieces (separated with waxed paper) and set aside.

5. Combine ½ cup (125 ml) water and remaining sugar in saucepan; bring to a boil to dissolve sugar. Cool to room temperature; flavor with rum to taste. Set aside.

6. Whip the cream until it holds stiff peaks. Fold into Chocolate Buttercream Icing.

7. To assemble, place first layer of cake on a plate. Brush one fourth of the rum syrup over cake. Spread a layer of icing evenly over cake. Place second cake layer on top; brush with syrup; spread with icing. Place the third layer of cake on top; brush with syrup and spread with icing. Place fourth layer of cake on top; brush with syrup and spread icing on top and long sides. Refrigerate until icing is firm.

8. To finish cake, trim a thin slice off each short end to reveal layers. Decorate with Chocolate Leaves and refrigerate. To serve, allow cake to stand at room temperature until icing softens slightly (about 1 hour).

Serves 8.

CHOCOLATE-RASPBERRY SWIRL CHEESECAKE

Tightly wrapped and stored in the freezer, this cheesecake will keep for two months, ready for unexpected guests or impromptu parties.

1¼ cups	flour	300 ml
3 tbl	sugar	3 tbl
¼ tsp	salt	¼ tsp
6 tbl	unsalted butter	6 tbl
6 oz	semisweet chocolate, coarsely chopped	170 g
2 lb	cream cheese, softened	900 g
1 cup	sugar	250 ml
5	eggs	5
3 tbl	flour	3 tbl
1 tsp	vanilla extract	1 tsp
4 tbl	raspberry liqueur	4 tbl
1 pint	fresh raspberries or 1 pound/450 g unsweetened frozen raspberries, unthawed	500 ml
¼ cup	currant jelly	60 ml

1. In a large bowl stir together flour, sugar, and salt. Cut in butter until mixture resembles coarse crumbs. Add enough water (about 2 tablespoons) to form a dough and chill 30 minutes.

2. Preheat oven to 350°F (175°C). Roll out dough and press into a 9-inch (22.5-cm) springform pan. Bake 12 minutes; remove from oven, and cool. Leave oven at 350°F (175°C) while preparing filling.

3. Heat chocolate over hot water in a double boiler until melted. In a mixing bowl beat cream cheese until smooth; gradually add sugar. Add eggs, one at a time, beating well after each addition. Stir in flour, vanilla, and 2 tablespoons of the raspberry liqueur.

4. Place two thirds of the cream cheese filling into crust. Stir melted chocolate and 1 cup (250 ml) of the raspberries into remaining filling. Divide chocolate-raspberry filling into sixths and drop by spoonfuls into the plain filling, then swirl with a knife to marble batter. Bake at 350°F (175°C) until top is set and center jiggles slightly if cake is gently shaken (70 minutes). Let cool in pan 1 hour, then remove from pan.

5. Chill 4–12 hours. Two hours before serving, heat currant jelly with remaining raspberry liqueur. Gently toss remaining raspberries with currant jelly glaze and arrange on top of cheesecake before serving.

Serves 10.

CHOCOLATE RUFFLE TORTE

Your efforts will be rewarded every time you make this stunning chocolate mousse torte.

¾ cup	unsalted butter, softened	175 ml
¾ cup	sugar	175 ml
¾ cup	finely ground almonds	175 ml
6 oz	bittersweet chocolate, melted and cooled	170 g
6	eggs, separated	6

Chocolate Mousse

1¼ cups	whipping cream	300 ml
7 tbl	sugar	7 tbl
4	egg yolks	4
6 oz	semisweet chocolate, melted and cooled	170 g
as needed	Chocolate Ribbon and Ruffles	as needed

(see page 77) or Chocolate Curls (see page 60)

1. Preheat oven to 350°F (175°C). Place circles of waxed paper in bottoms of two buttered and lightly floured 8-inch (20-cm) round cake pans.

2. In a large mixing bowl, cream butter with half of the sugar until light and fluffy. Add almonds and beat well. Beat in melted chocolate.

3. Add the 6 egg yolks, one at a time, beating well after each addition; beat until fluffy.

4. In a separate bowl beat the 6 egg whites until soft peaks form. Gradually add remaining sugar and beat until stiff but still glossy.

5. Stir one fourth of the egg whites into the chocolate mixture to lighten batter. Gently fold in remaining whites.

6. Divide the batter equally between the two pans and gently smooth top of batter. Bake until set (about 30–40 minutes). Cool in pans 10 minutes, then turn out onto wire racks to finish cooling. This cake tends to sink in the middle as it cools. If necessary trim top with serrated knife to create even layers.

7. While cake is baking prepare Chocolate Mousse. Whip the cream until soft peaks form and refrigerate. Combine ½ cup (125 ml) water and sugar in saucepan. Bring to a boil to dissolve sugar; boil 1 minute. Measure out ½ cup (125 ml) hot syrup. Place the 4 egg yolks in a deep stainless steel bowl or top of double boiler. Whisk in hot syrup over boiling water until the mixture holds soft peaks (5–7 minutes). Remove yolks from heat and beat until they are cool. Stir in melted chocolate. Fold in one eighth of the whipped cream. Gradually fold in remaining whipped cream. If you fold the cream in too quickly, the chocolate will harden and form chocolate chips.

8. Place one of the cake layers on a plate. Spread half the mousse over this layer. Set second layer on top of mousse. Spread remaining mousse on sides and top of cake. Refrigerate until mousse is firm (about 45 minutes).

9. Decorate cake with Chocolate Ribbon and Ruffles, or sprinkle top with Chocolate Curls.

Serves 8.

Making Chocolate Ruffles and Ribbons

With a little practice you can make chocolate ruffles and ribbons for decorating tortes like the one on page 75.

1. For ruffles, refrigerate a marble slab or baking sheet for 30 minutes. Pour an inch-wide (2.5-cm) strip of tempered chocolate (see page 29) onto chilled marble and spread into a thin, smooth sheet 3 by 10 inches (7.5 by 25 cm).

2. When chocolate begins to set but is still pliable, use a spatula to push sheet of chocolate from right to left. With left hand gather chocolate into a ruffle as you go along. Transfer ruffle to a pan lined with waxed paper, cover with plastic film, and refrigerate until ready to use. Make enough ruffles to decorate top of torte.

3. For ribbon, cut a sheet of waxed paper slightly wider than the cake is tall and slightly longer than the cake's circumference. With a spatula, spread a thin layer of melted, tempered chocolate onto the waxed paper. When the chocolate begins to set but is still pliable, place one end of the ribbon of chocolate against the cake, with layer of chocolate facing in, and wrap smoothly against sides of cake. Press top edge of chocolate ribbon onto top of cake. Refrigerate until firm and waxed paper pulls away easily.

DEVIL'S FOOD CAKE

This recipe makes a rich, dark layer cake (see cover photo).

¾ cup	unsweetened cocoa	175 ml
¾ cup	boiling water	175 ml
½ cup	shortening or butter	125 ml
2 cups	sugar	500 ml
2	eggs	2
1 tsp	vanilla extract	1 tsp
¼ tsp	salt	¼ tsp
1½ tsp	baking soda	1½ tsp
1 cup	buttermilk	250 ml
2 cups	sifted cake flour	500 ml
2 recipes	Chocolate Buttercream Icing (see page 34)	2 recipes

1. Preheat oven to 350°F (175°C). Line bottoms of two 8-inch (20-cm) round cake pans with circles of parchment paper. Lightly oil and flour pans and paper. Dissolve cocoa in the boiling water. Set aside.

2. In a bowl cream together shortening and sugar until fluffy. Add eggs, one at a time, beating well after each addition. Beat in vanilla and salt.

3. Stir baking soda into buttermilk. To egg mixture add ½ cup (125 ml) of the flour and ⅓ cup (85 ml) of the buttermilk mixture; beat well. Add remaining flour and buttermilk alternately, beating well after each addition. Stir in cocoa mixture.

4. Pour batter into prepared pans. Bake until top of cake springs back when gently pressed with finger and a toothpick inserted into center comes out clean (30–35 minutes). Cool in pans 5 minutes, then turn out onto wire racks and cool completely. Ice with Chocolate Buttercream Icing.

Serves 8.

CHOCOLATE CHEESECAKE CUM LAUDE

Chantilly Cream (see page 80) makes an exquisite topping for this phenomenal cheesecake when strawberries aren't in season.

1 recipe	Chocolate Cookie Crust (see page 48)	1 recipe
12 oz	semisweet chocolate, coarsely chopped	350 g
24 oz	cream cheese	680 g
1 cup	sugar	250 ml
⅛ tsp	salt	⅛ tsp
1½ tsp	vanilla extract	1½ tsp
3	eggs	3
1 cup	sour cream	250 ml
1 pt	strawberries, sliced in half	450 g

1. Prepare crust and press into bottom and up sides of a 10-inch (25-cm) springform pan. Wrap outside of pan with plastic film and then foil. Set aside.

2. Preheat oven to 325°F (160°C). Melt chocolate in the top of a double boiler over low heat. Stir until completely melted and smooth. Remove from heat and set aside to cool slightly.

3. In a large mixing bowl beat cream cheese until smooth. Add sugar, salt, and vanilla. Beat well until smooth. Add chocolate and mix. Add eggs, one at a time, beating well after each addition. Add sour cream and beat until smooth. Pour filling into prepared pan and smooth top. Set pan in a larger pan containing an inch (2.5 cm) of water.

4. Bake in water bath until center jiggles but is no longer liquid and the edges are dry (1–1¼ hours). Carefully remove pan to rack to cool; cover and refrigerate several hours or overnight.

5. Remove cake from springform pan, top with strawberries, and serve.

Serves 12.

CHOCOLATE MOUSSE TORTE

Everyone loves chocolate mousse, especially when it's encased in a chocolate cookie-crumb crust. The torte must chill at least fours hours, or overnight, so it's an excellent choice to make ahead for a party.

1 recipe	Chocolate Cookie Crust (see page 48)	1 recipe
1 recipe	Chocolate Mousse (see page 74)	1 recipe

Chantilly Cream

½ cup	whipping cream	125 ml
1 tbl	sifted confectioner's sugar	1 tbl
¼ tsp	vanilla extract or 1 teaspoon liqueur	¼ tsp

as needed	Chocolate Curls (see page 60), for garnish (optional)	as needed

1. Preheat oven to 350°F (175°C). Prepare crust in an 8-inch (20-cm) springform pan. Bake according to instructions. Cool and refrigerate.

2. Prepare Chocolate Mousse; do not chill, but pour into chilled shell. Refrigerate pie at least 4 hours or overnight.

3. About 30 minutes before serving, chill the cream, mixing bowl, and beaters (or whisk) before whipping the cream. Whip the cream until it begins to thicken; add sugar and vanilla or liqueur. Continue beating until soft peaks form.

4. To serve, remove torte from springform pan, pipe spirals of Chantilly Cream around edge, and sprinkle cream with Chocolate Curls, if desired.

Serves 8.

NOT GUILTY

The verdict is unanimous. The irresistible selections in this section demonstrate beyond a doubt that you can splurge on chocolate with a clear conscience. These tantalizing recipes are for nutrition-minded chocolate lovers who want great-tasting treats without excessive amounts of dietary fat, cholesterol, or calories.

CHOCOLATE MADELEINE
ICE CREAM SANDWICHES

These thoroughly adult ice cream sandwiches require madeleine pans for molding the cookies. This batter is thicker than the traditional madeleine batter, resulting in a denser cookie, capable of holding the ice cream in a sandwich.

1	egg yolk	1
½ cup	sugar	125 ml
½ cup	unsweetened cocoa	125 ml
½ cup	flour, sifted	125 ml
1 tsp	baking powder	1 tsp
pinch	salt	pinch
2 tbl	unsalted butter, softened	2 tbl
1 tsp	vanilla extract	1 tsp
3	egg whites	3
1 pint	ice milk, any flavor	500 ml

1. Preheat oven to 425°F (220°C). Butter 2 madeleine pans (for 24 cookies). In a medium bowl beat together egg yolk and sugar until well mixed. Whisk in cocoa. In another bowl combine flour, baking powder, and salt. Fold flour mixture into yolk mixture, then fold in butter and vanilla.

2. Whisk egg whites until stiff peaks form. Fold into batter. Fill each mold two thirds full. Bake until madeleines are firm to the touch (10–15 minutes). Remove from pan and let cool on wire racks.

3. Using an oval ice cream scoop, place 1 scoop ice milk on flat side of a cooled madeleine. Place another madeleine, flat side down, on top. Press together gently. Repeat with remaining madeleines. Wrap individual sandwiches tightly and freeze.

Makes 12 ice cream sandwiches, 12 servings.
Each serving: cal 118, fat 4 g, cal from fat 28%, chol 26 mg

DOUBLE-CHOCOLATE CRÊPES

Serve this very sophisticated dessert to very special guests.

Chocolate Crêpes

½ cup	skim milk	125 ml
2	eggs	2
1 tsp	vanilla extract	1 tsp
¼ tsp	salt	¼ tsp
1 cup	flour	250 ml
1 oz	semisweet chocolate, finely chopped	30 g
2 tbl	unsalted butter, softened	2 tbl
1 quart	chocolate ice milk	900 ml
as needed	orange marmalade	as needed
1 recipe	Bittersweet Chocolate Sauce (see page 20), for topping (optional)	1 recipe
⅔ cup	whipped light cream, for topping (optional)	150 ml
as needed	unsweetened cocoa, for dusting (optional)	as needed

1. In a food processor or blender, mix ½ cup (125 ml) cold water, milk, eggs, vanilla, and salt. Add flour and mix well. Place mixture in a bowl; cover. Set aside in a cool spot at least 4 hours or refrigerate overnight. (If mixture is refrigerated, bring to room temperature before proceeding.)

2. In the top of a double boiler or in a bowl set over barely simmering water, melt chocolate and butter together. Cool to room temperature.

3. In a small bowl thoroughly blend chocolate mixture with egg mixture.

4. Heat a seasoned crêpe pan or a lightly buttered frying pan over medium-high heat. Pour in a small ladleful of batter. Quickly roll and turn the pan to spread the batter. Pour any

excess batter back into bowl. Cook crêpe until dark brown specks appear on top, then turn crêpe over briefly to cook the other side. Cool. Repeat with remaining batter to make 12 crêpes. Stack crêpes, separating them with waxed paper or plastic film so they will not stick together.

5. To assemble, roll each crêpe around 1 scoop of ice milk. Place rolled crêpes on dessert plates. Spoon orange marmalade to the side of each crêpe. Top with Bittersweet Chocolate Sauce or whipped light cream lightly dusted with cocoa, if desired.

Makes 12 servings.
Each serving: cal 276, fat 6 g, cal from fat 17%, chol 47 mg

CHOCOLATE-PECAN MERINGUES

Clouds of chocolate meringue perch atop pecan halves to make these delicate cookies (see photo on page 17). Lining the baking sheets with parchment paper will make it easier to remove the cookies.

2	egg whites	2
¼ tsp	cream of tartar	¼ tsp
⅛ tsp	salt	⅛ tsp
⅔ cup	sugar	150 ml
1 tsp	vanilla extract	1 tsp
3 tbl	unsweetened cocoa	3 tbl
48	small pecan halves	48

1. Line baking sheets with parchment paper. Preheat oven to 300°F (150°C).

2. In a mixing bowl combine egg whites, cream of tartar, and salt. Beat at high speed until foamy. Gradually add sugar, beating until egg-white mixture is stiff and glossy.

3. Reduce speed and beat in vanilla and cocoa until cocoa is completely incorporated.

4. Drop rounded teaspoonfuls of batter 2 inches (5 cm) apart on parchment-lined baking sheet. Tuck two pecan halves partway into the base of each mound of batter. Bake until meringues are firm to the touch (25–30 minutes). Remove to wire racks to cool.

Makes 24 cookies, 24 servings.
Each serving: cal 40, fat 2 g, cal from fat 35%, chol 0 mg

Chocolate Sorbet

Chocolate lovers will welcome this light, refreshing dessert on those hot summer nights.

¾ cup	unsweetened cocoa	175 ml
½ cup	sugar	125 ml
pinch	salt	pinch
1¾ cups	skim milk	425 ml
1½ tsp	vanilla extract	1½ tsp

1. In a medium saucepan combine cocoa, sugar, and salt; mix well. Gradually stir in milk. Bring just to a boil over moderate heat, stirring constantly. Reduce heat and simmer 5 minutes, still stirring.

2. Remove from heat and let cool. Add vanilla. Transfer to an ice cream machine and freeze according to manufacturer's instructions.

Makes 1½ pints (700 ml), 6 servings.
Each serving: cal 115, fat 2 g, cal from fat 11%, chol 1 mg

Plating and Serving Tips

The way you serve your chocolate creations can dramatically enhance their presentation. Choose a serving dish or tray that contributes to the overall effect, whether casual, whimsical, or formal. Plate the item attractively, centering it on the serving dish and removing any stray crumbs or drips.

The way you slice cakes, tortes, and other desserts for serving is also important. Depending on what you're serving, use a scoop, serving spatula, or sharp knife. A serrated knife often works best for cakes and tortes; scrape the knife clean after each cut, or dip it into warm water. Finally, if there are edible decorations, try to include some in each serving.

CHOCOLATE WAFFLES

With or without nuts, these chocolaty waffles make a wonderful low-fat base for ice cream and sauces.

1½ cups	flour	350 ml
¼ cup	unsweetened cocoa	60 ml
1 tsp	baking powder	1 tsp
1 tsp	baking soda	1 tsp
⅓ cup	sugar	85 ml
2¼ cups	buttermilk	550 ml
¼ cup	oil	60 ml
1 tsp	vanilla extract	1 tsp
4	eggs whites	4
pinch	cream of tartar	pinch
1 cup	chopped pecans (optional)	250 ml

1. Sift together flour, cocoa, baking powder, baking soda, and sugar. Make well in center.

2. In a separate bowl mix buttermilk, oil, and vanilla. Pour into the well and mix with dry ingredients.

3. Beat egg whites with cream of tartar until soft peaks form. Gradually fold into batter, one third at a time. Fold in pecans, if used.

4. Cook in waffle iron according to manufacturer's instructions. Serve warm or at room temperature.

Makes 6 waffles, 6 servings.
Each serving: cal 295, fat 11 g, cal from fat 32%, chol 3 mg

CHOCOLATE-SWIRLED BABKAS

Topped with streusel and bursting with fudgy cocoa filling, these sweet loaves are a New York bakery favorite.

Cocoa Filling

⅓ cup	unsweetened cocoa	85 ml
⅔ cup	sugar	150 ml

Streusel Topping

2 tbl	butter, softened	2 tbl
¼ tsp	ground cinnamon	¼ tsp
⅓ cup	confectioners' sugar	85 ml
¼ cup	flour	60 ml

2 pkgs	active dry yeast	2 pkgs
½ cup	warm (105°F/41°C) water	125 ml
⅓ cup	sugar	85 ml
⅔ cup	warm (105°F/41°C) skim milk	150 ml
½ tsp each	salt and vanilla extract	½ tsp each
4 tbl	butter, softened	4 tbl
4½ cups	flour	1 l
3	eggs	3
1 cup	coarsely chopped walnuts (optional)	250 ml

1. In a small bowl mix cocoa and sugar until well combined and no lumps remain. Set aside.

2. In a medium bowl beat butter with cinnamon until fluffy; gradually beat in sugar, then mix in flour until crumbly and uniformly combined. Set aside.

3. In a large mixing bowl sprinkle yeast over the water. Add 1 teaspoon sugar. Let stand until yeast is soft (about 5 minutes). Mix in remaining sugar, milk, salt, vanilla, and 2 tablespoons of the butter.

4. Add 2½ cups (600 ml) of the flour. Mix to blend, then beat at medium speed until smooth and elastic (about 5 minutes). Separate one of the eggs; reserve white for glaze. Beat in egg yolk and remaining whole eggs, one at a time. Stir in about 1½ cups (350 ml) more flour to make a soft dough.

5. Turn dough out onto a floured surface, kneading until smooth and satiny (10–12 minutes), adding just enough flour to prevent dough from being sticky. Turn dough in an oiled bowl. Cover with plastic film and a towel; let rise in a warm place until doubled in bulk (45–60 minutes). Place dough on a lightly floured surface and punch down. Cover with inverted bowl and let rest for 10 minutes. Melt remaining butter. Set aside.

6. Divide dough in half. Roll out each half on a lightly floured surface to a 10- by 20-inch (25- by 50-cm) rectangle. Brush 1 tablespoon of the melted butter over each rectangle, leaving about a ½-inch (1.25-cm) margin on all edges. Sprinkle half of the Cocoa Filling over buttered surface of each rectangle, then sprinkle with ½ cup (125 ml) walnuts, if used.

7. Starting with a 20-inch (50-cm) side, roll each rectangle of dough tightly, jelly-roll style. Pinch edge to seal.

8. Carefully place the rolls into 2 well-oiled 4½- by 8½-inch (11.25- by 21.25-cm) loaf pans, zigzagging the rolls to fit.

9. Let rise until almost doubled in bulk (35–45 minutes). Preheat oven to 350°F (175°C). Beat reserved egg white with 1 teaspoon water; brush egg white mixture over loaves. Sprinkle each loaf with half of the Streusel Topping.

10. Bake until coffee cakes are well browned (30–35 minutes). Carefully remove loaves from pans and let cool on wire racks. Slice each cake into 10 slices.

Makes 20 servings.
Each serving: cal 206, fat 5 g, cal from fat 20%, chol 41 mg

ITALIAN BOMBE

Few frozen presentations convey festivity as readily as a glistening, multi-layered bombe. This very impressive—and delicious—bombe contains two ice milk layers and a layer of pear sorbet.

The classic lidded bombe mold is made of tinned steel and looks like a football that has been halved lengthwise, but for this recipe you can use any 1½ quart- (1.4 l-) mold or even smaller molds for individual servings. Chilling the mold before filling it with the first layer of ice cream, and packing successive layers firmly to eliminate air pockets help ensure a silken finish when the bombe is unmolded for serving.

Bombes can be prepared up to the point of garnishing as much as a day before you serve them, but the quality deteriorates if they are held longer than about 24 hours. You can garnish the finished bombe, if desired, with whipped light cream and chocolate shavings.

Pear Sorbet

⅓ cup	sugar	85 ml
2 tbl	lemon juice	2 tbl
1 tbl	pear-flavored liqueur	1 tbl
1 tsp	grated lemon zest	1 tsp
1 can (29 oz)	pear halves, packed in natural juice or water, drained, puréed, and chilled	1 can (850 ml)
1 pint each	chocolate and vanilla ice milk	500 ml each
as needed	whipped light cream and chocolate shavings, for garnish (optional)	as needed

1. In a small saucepan heat sugar with ⅓ cup (85 ml) water until sugar melts. Remove from heat and cool. Add lemon juice, liqueur, and lemon zest. Chill. Stir sugar syrup into chilled purée. Transfer to an ice cream machine and freeze according to manufacturer's instructions. Let sorbet "ripen" in freezer for several hours.

2. Chill a 1½-quart (1.4-l) bombe mold in the freezer for several hours or overnight. Brush the inside of the mold with oil and line it with two 1-inch-wide (2.5-cm-wide) strips of aluminum foil or waxed paper crisscrossed and extending 3 inches (7.5 cm) above the rim of the mold at both ends.

3. Press three quarters of the chocolate ice milk into the mold, evenly covering the sides and bottom. Freeze until firm.

4. Press the vanilla ice milk into an even layer over the chocolate ice milk. Freeze until very firm.

5. Fill in the center of the bombe with the Pear Sorbet. Freeze until very firm.

6. Cover the top surface with the remaining chocolate ice milk. Cover with plastic film and freeze overnight or until ice milk is very firm.

7. To unmold, invert the frozen bombe onto a serving plate. Cover the mold with a hot towel. To help loosen the bombe, pull gently on the aluminum foil strips. Decorate the bombe with whipped cream and chocolate shavings, if desired.

Serves 12.
Each serving: cal 112, fat 2 g, cal from fat 16%, chol 6 mg

CABERNET AND CHOCOLATE

Wine and chocolate may seem like an odd couple if you've never tried them together, but the rouge-et-noir combination can be quite pleasing to the eye and the palate. Bittersweet chocolate goes especially well with Cabernet Sauvignon. Strong, aromatic, slightly bitter, and astringent, the dry red wine—like a cup of dark-roast coffee—offers a satisfying balance to the equally intense flavor of the chocolate.

INDEX